# The Home-Based Business Guide

- planning a business
- choosing an entity
- IRS approved tax deductions

Laura Lynn Burke, EA

The Home-Based Business Guide
- planning a business
- choosing an entity
- IRS approved tax deductions

Professional Tax Masters, Inc.
328 E. Lincoln Highway
New Lenox, IL. 60451
www.Professionaltaxmasters.com
www.Lauralynnburke.com
708-969-2229

Cover design by Lorelei Productions

To order the book:
www.Professionaltaxmasters.com or www.Lauralynnburke.com

*Library of Congress Cataloging Publication Data*
Unassigned
Burke, Laura
   Home-Based business & Taxes
   Includes Index
1.Home-Based Business  2. Taxes  3. Networking  4. Lynn, Laura
5. Sole Proprietorship  6. Corporations  7. Partnerships
8. Limited Liability Companies

 Title:  The Home-Based Business Guide; planning a business, choosing an entity and IRS approved tax deductions.

Disclaimer: All material was assumed correct as provided.  Author accepts no liability for misinformation.
Printed in the USA

# Planning a Business....

**The Home-Based Business Guide:**
**Planning a business**

**What type of product or service do I feel comfortable marketing?**

**Do I believe in the products or services?**

**How many others are marketing the same product/service? In what manner are they marketing them?**

**What are start up costs?**

**Will there be future start-up costs or ongoing fees?**

**How will the above costs be paid?**

**What type of working environment do you need?**

**What type of supplies will I need?**

**How much will my supplies cost?**

**Do I need to carry an inventory?**
**If I do need to carry an inventory what is the shelf life of the product?**

**Can I afford to pay cash for these products?**

**Forms of Ownership**

## The Home-Based Business Guide:
### Planning a business

*What the wise do in the beginning, fools do in the end.*

Do you own a home based business, or are you considering owning a home-based business. Knowing the tax benefits may assist you in planning your move wisely, or preparing your taxes accordingly. Most home-based businesses are run as sole-proprietorships, where all business income and loss is shown on an IRS Schedule C of your personal 1040 tax returns. One of the benefits of owning a home-based business is losses you incur as a sole proprietorship carry through to W2 income.

Let's look at an example: As a salaried professional making 75,000.00 a year, opens a small home-based business and has additional income from home-based business of $12,000.00 for first year in business, but the business also has a loss of $14,500.00. The $14,500.00 loss first goes against the income from the home-based business (12,000.00) and then any difference (2500.00) will go against income from W2 wages (75,000.00-2500 = 72500.00). Thus reducing taxes normally paid on the W2 income. This is one reason many people venture into a home-based business is for the deductions.

The home based business must be a legitimate business. The business must be run like a business not a hobby, and should show a profit some time during the first five years. I will explain in detail as we go through the process of becoming a legitimate home-based business.

Owning your own business is an "American Dream" of many. With today's economic issues, foreclosures, job cuts and downsizing owning a home based business never looked so good! Many are looking more closely at becoming business owners. It is the easiest way to start a business is a home-based business.

Many successful "corporate world" people have been extremely successful in quitting their day job to run wildly profitable home-based businesses. Many start out part-time and grow into full time. The IRS doesn't care if it is a part-time business as long as it is run professional and legitimately as a business it can be tax deductible. Many new entrepreneurs will be made during this paradigm shift.

IDC, a top national research firm believes there are approximately 35 million home offices households in the United Sates. The successful rate for a home-based business is 70% will last over three years according to the home-based business institute. Entrepreneur's magazine estimates that 427 billion dollars is generated each year by home-based businesses. Home based business owners are averaging $63.000.00 and more in income a year based on IDC statistics. The SBA's Office of Advocacy shows that in 2000 nearly 20,000 entrepreneurs grossed more than one million dollars operating from home-based businesses. That is a huge documented success story.

With that amount of income potential many are taking hard looks at direct marketing home- based businesses. If you are one of the many and have done your home-work, you know what business venture you're going to start, you've asked yourself all the above questions. You are ready to start.

Many people are contemplating starting their own home-based business but never do because they are unsure of what steps to take, the correct process and just how to go about it. It can be an overwhelming projet with out proper quideance, but with the proper quidance it can be simplified and the process made easier. I hope you will find the guidance you've been waiting for in, *"The Home-Based Business Guide."* Here are the ins, the outs and the inside info you need when starting a home-based business.

Your first step is to plan ahead. Plan before you commit. Having a plan and knowing what you want to do and how to do it is the key initial step any business owner should adapt. Having a plan to follow will insure a more successful outcome than those without a plan.

Failure to plan can cost you serious money and headaches in the future. Planning reduces financial risk as well as providing written proof if questioned or audited by the IRS that you are in business to make a profit vs. a business being worked as a hobby. This will be discussed in detail later.

Planning involves the following questions, ask yourself:

**What type of product or service do I feel comfortable marketing?**

Everyone feels differently about products and services. We all feel strongly about those that we can identify with, those that we believe in. Look for a company that has products you may be familiar with or feel strongly about.

**Do I believe in the products or services?**

Your conviction alone will help you sell. You need to believe in the product and the company, when you believe others will to!

**How many others are marketing the same product/service? In what manner are they marketing them?**

This is a two fold question, first is the market already saturated with marketers of the product/service, if so is the company you are looking at innovative with their marketing plans and concept. Do you think it is a marketable concept?

**What are start up costs?**

As a new business you can deduct up to $5000.00 in business start-up costs such as license fees, advertising costs, professional fees (accounting, attorney and tax professionals), office supplies and market research.

**Will there be future start-up costs or ongoing fees?**

Cost for additional products, marketing material, training and/or inventory. Inventory is not a deductible start up cost. Marketing materials and training would be considered in the start up costs during the first year.

**How will the above costs be paid?**

Will they be paid out of future commissions, or are they to be paid immediately upon starting. Do you have the cash to put in to the business or will you need to use credit?

**What type of working environment do you need?**

Will a home office work, a cell phone vs. a land line. Do you need a standard office away from home? These are important questions to know the answers to before committing to a business. It gives you a better grasp as to the cost needed to get started.

**What type of supplies will I need?**

Examples of such supplies might be office furniture, a computer, a lap top, printer, fax, phone lines, supplies and such. We will discuss the use of Section 179 deductions for business owners. Many of the larger items such as office furniture, equipment, and new this year computers may be added to the Section 179 deduction. We will go into greater detail as we discuss deductions for business owners.

**How much will my supplies cost?**

Do I have the money now to invest to get started correctly? With the new computer deduction added to the 179 deductions it maybe the best time to purchase a new computer for your business.

**Do I need to carry an inventory?**
If so how much do I need to maintain in my inventory on an on going bases.

**If I do need to carry an inventory what is the shelf life of the product?**

Some examples, make-up with Mary Kay vs. an acia berry juice product, each have a different shelf life. Other products may have a timeless shelf life like jewelry products.

**Can I afford to pay cash for these products?**

If not is a credit card an acceptable means of starting my inventory.

If starting with credit have a plan in place to pay off the credit so you may use it again and the interest doesn't eat into your profits.

Once you have a business you can identify with chosen, you will need to consider what type of business entity do you want to be?

**Forms of Ownership**

One of the first decisions that you will need to make is how your company should be structured. The decision is an important one that will have long-term implications. If you are going into business with another individual or group then this must be discussed in the very beginning. Discussing your options with a tax professional, such as an Enrolled Agent, Attorney or CPA is important in selecting the form of ownership that is right for your business. Some things to consider when making that choice:

- What is the plan both short term and long term for your new business

- What is the type (nature) and size of your business, now and in the future

- Who has what control; borrowing money, day to day activities, expanding, products,
  - inventory, marketing, sales and service

- What type of business structure you are comfortable with

- What is your need for cash out of the business

- Will you want to reinvest earnings into the business.

- Consider business & asset protection, vulnerability to lawsuits

- .

- Expected profit (or loss) of the business

- Tax implications of the different business entity structures

# Choosing a Business Entity.....

- **Sole Proprietorship**
- **Corporation C or S**
- **Partnership: General or Limited Liability**
- **LLC or LLP or Series LLC**

**The Home-Based Business Guide:**
**Choosing a Business Entity**

You can choose from a sole proprietorship, Limited Liability Co. known as an LLC, a corporation or a partnership. You should determine which suits your needs best, based on the advantages and disadvantages for liability protection as well as tax related advantageous and disadvantages.

**Sole Proprietorships**

Most small businesses start-out as sole proprietorships. A sole-proprietorship is designed only for one person. Married couples can elect to be taxed like a sole proprietorship; each spouse must file their own IRS schedule C as well as their own schedule SE for reporting Social Security and Medicare. By filing this way you both get credit for Social Security and Medicare taxes. The two of you must be the only owners and you both must actively participate in the business.

You, either as an individual or married couple are responsible for all day-to-day responsibilities for operating your business. Sole proprietors own all the assets of the business and the profits generated by it. They also assume complete responsibility for any of its liabilities or debts. A sole proprietorship gives the least amount of protection from a liability stand point. There is

no separation between the business and you. You and the business are viewed as one in the same, so the businesses liabilities are yours. In the eyes of the law and the public, you are one in the same.
If you should die, the business would cease to exist, unless originally operated with a surviving spouse.

As for taxes your income is added in on your 1040 with the use of a schedule C. Your losses are also carried to the 1040 from the schedule C thus allowing your losses to carry over against any W2 income you may have. This is considered a pass through entity, because your income and losses are being passed through to your 1040. Most business deductions are allowed for sole proprietorships. Because of this many home-based businesses choose to be sole proprietorships.

There is no cost to become a sole proprietorship, no documents to file. You should check with your city or village to obtain a business license for working from your home. The cost is typically nominal around $15.00 TO $25.00 or so, but it is the correct way to start a business and again it shows you are in business to be in business, vs. being viewed as a hobby.

When opening a bank account, if you re not using your own name for the name of your business most will request you file an assumed name certificate with the county. The cost is around five to ten dollars. They then require that you run an ad in a local paper for two to three weeks announcing your new business and name. Then the bank will open your business checking account for you with your assumed business name. This is a very simple procedure that makes your business legitimate.

Advantages of a Sole Proprietorship (You)

- The easiest, quickest and least expensive form of ownership.
- You are in complete control and make all decisions.
- You receive all income and losses generated by the business.
- Profits from the business flow directly to your 1040 (Personal tax return)
- The business may be dissolved and closed easily.
- Upon death your business doesn't exist anymore. (Unless operated by a surviving spouse)

Disadvantages of a Sole Proprietorship (You)

- You have unlimited liability and are legally responsible for all debts against the business.
- Both your business and personal assets are at risk.
- You could be at a disadvantage when obtaining funds or loans, most often limited to using

your own personal savings or consumer loans (personal credit cards or home equity loans.)

- Some employee benefits like owner's medical insurance premiums are not directly deductible from business income (only partially deductible as an adjustment to income).

Federal Tax Forms for Sole Proprietorship

- Form 1040: Individual Income Tax Return
- Schedule C: Profit or Loss from Business
- Schedule SE: Self-Employment Tax
- Form 1040-ES: Estimated Tax for Individuals
- Form 4562: Depreciation and Amortization
- Form 8829: Expenses for Business Use of your Home
- Employment Tax Forms

**Limited Liability Company (LLC)**

A Limited Liability Company is a relatively new type of business entity that is permissible in most states. It is designed to provide the limited liability features of a corporation and the tax benefits and flexibility of a partnership. The limited liability company, LLC is very similar to a sole proprietorship because its owners all jointly own the business and participate in the profits and losses together. The LLC will be taxed as a partnership.

15

The owners of an LLC are members, and the duration of the LLC is determined when the organization papers are filed. The time can be extended by a vote of the members at the time of expiration or prior to. LLC's cannot have more than two of the four characteristics that define corporations: Limited liability to the extent of the LLC's assets, perpetual life, centralization of management, and free transferability of ownership interests, or the LLC will be taxed as a corporation.

An LLC is organized with a document, "articles of organization" or "the rules of organization" determined by each state. It is also common to have an operating agreement among the member s to prevent future disputes. This document shows the members of the LLC, the governing member's management, operations and distribution of income.

The LLC does offer the owners/member some protection for the liabilities of the company vs. their own. Limited Liability companies are treated like a sole proprietorship for tax purposes.

Professional Limited Liability Company PLLC is similar to the LLC; it is organized for the purpose pf providing professional services. Most often used in professions that the state requires licensure to provide services, such as a doctor, chiropractor, lawyer, accountant, architect, engineer or tax professional.

Series LLC

A series LLC is a single limited liability company that has multiple series, mini-cells mirroring an LLC. Each cell is allowed to have separate managers, members, operating agreements, and all are individual and separate for liability purposes.

LLC's have been in existence since 1996 in Delaware; recently they have been approved in six more states, Oklahoma, Iowa, Illinois, Nevada, Tennessee and Utah.

For the Secretary of State filing purposes the series LLC is considered one entity. In forming an LLC series, first an LLC (master LLC) is formed just the same as an LLC, you need to file Articles of organization for all states other than Delaware. Delaware requires you to file a Certificate of Formation.

When forming an LLC a form LLC-5-5 is used, when forming an LLC Series a Form LLC 5-5(S) is used. In Illinois there is a $500.00 filing fee for an LLC, for an LLC Series it is $750.00 for the master company and $50.00 for each unit added to the series. This is significantly lower than forming all individual corporations or even all LLC's on their own.

Another advantage is the annual renewal fee of $250.00 for the master cell and $50.00 for each additional one. This could save you a bundle if compared to $250.00 for each cell. What if you have ten cells or units that would cost $500.00 for all ten vs. $2500.00 to renew ten.

Other advantages are the liability protection, that each cell is treated as a separate entity. Each cell can hold title to property, make purchase transactions, borrower money, sue and be sued, etc in each cells own name.

Illinois requires each cell to contain the name of the master cell plus their name. For example ABC LLC is the master company, and ABC Series 1, ABC Series 2.

Being from Illinois I used Illinois as an example, however each state has their own rules and statues.

Most often LLC Series are created when multiple properties are owned; forming a separate LLC's to own each property or business entity. This way multiple owners can participate in each property, the owners of the master cell do not need to have an interest in each unit.. In the case of a law suit, only the LLC holding the property would be involved thus protecting all others.

Disadvantageous are that it is new and has not been tested in bankruptcy court. Nick Marsico author of the article, Current Status of the Series LLC: Illinois Series LLC Improves Upon Delaware Series, Nov 2006 states, "As of now, there is no ruling one way or another whether the separateness of each cell will be acknowledged in court. The bankruptcy code states that any person may be a debtor. The definition of "person" includes individuals, partnerships and corporations. LLC's are not included in the list. Case law has made it clear that the list is not exclusive."

The draw back is the time and money involved to create each one and maintain each one with tax returns.

In 2008, Series LLC was given a boost with the release of IRS Private Ruling Letter 200803004, which clarified and determined that Series LLC's are permitted to use the same "check the box" tax clarification as all other entities.

What this means is that you are able to elect a different tax classification for each unit (cell) in the series LLC. Each cell will have its Tax ID number.

Advantageous of an Limited Liability Company

- No annual Meeting required

- No board of directors

- Pass through entity, profit and loss flows through to member's personal tax return

- Profits are taxed personally at the member's tax base.

- The LLC owners are protected to some degree for any and all debts beyond the capacity of the entity

- Member's interests can be assigned without transferring the title to the membership interest

Disadvantageous of a Limited Liability Company

- Many states such as: Alabama, California, Kentucky, New Jersey, New York, Pennsylvania. Tennessee, and Texas, impose a franchise tax on LLC's. Texas has what they call a "margin tax" same thing as a franchise tax. The franchise fee is the fee charged by the state to be an LLC. The tax can be based on revenue, profits, number of owners, or the amount of capital employed be the state, can also be a combination of any of these.

- Due to the newness of LLC's not all states recognize it inn the same manner as corporations for liability purposes.

- Cannot be owned by a corporation, would be considered an incorporated branch and double taxes.

You will need to discuss the pros and cons with your professional tax planner based on you and your personal and businesses plan. Keep in mind, that outside of the seven states that have accepted the LLC Series the other states have not. Therefore it is not a guaranty that the series of cells will provide the liability protection you need. It may and there is always the chance it may not.

It has been agrued in tax court many times, and the tax court has consistently ruled that as long as certain rules are followed, each unit (cell) will be treated as a separate entity and taxed accordingly. Theredore it is believed that if you put your LLC Series together correctly and follow the rules, it should be treated in the same manner.

Federal Tax Forms for LLC

Depending on the way you choose to operate your LLC your tax forms will be based accordingly. With a single owner, profits and losses are shown on a schedule C just like the sole proprietorship. If more than one owner, the LLC, is then viewed as a partnership. The LLC must use the IRS 1065 Partnership Form for taxes.

The LLC must also utilize the IRS Schedule K1, Partners Share of Income, Credits, Deductions, etc. showing its member's allocations of profits, losses credits and deductions. A copy is given to each member for calculating income or loss to be reported on their schedule E, Supplemental Income and Loss, along with their 1040 personal tax return. The schedule E flows through to the 1040, thus making a limited liability company a pass through entity as well.

A Limited Liability Company may elect to be taxed as a corporation by filing IRS Form 8832, or if you have two or more members and do not file the above form 8832 the LLC will be treated as a partnership. If only one owner you will be treated as a sole proprietorship when filing taxes you will use a schedule C.

An LLC is not required to hold an annual meeting. LLC's can be owned by one or more individuals, a Corporation or a partnership. Unless specified, members own a proportionate share, which can be divided any way chosen.

When opening a bank account in the LLC's name copies of your "articles of organization" or "the rules of organization" will be required.

You will also need to file for a city or village business license.

LLC's are becoming the preferred entity for both small and home-based businesses, when not in one of the franchise-fee states because they are a more flexible form of ownership, easier to administer and quicker to open. Members of an LLC can also split profits and losses any way they choose.

**Corporations**

A corporation is chartered by the state in which it is incorporated is considered by law to be a separate entity, apart from those who own it. A corporation can be taxed, and sued, and it can enter into contractual agreements. The owners of a corporation are its shareholders. The shareholders elect a board of directors to administer the major policies and decisions. The corporation has a life of its own and does not dissolve when ownership changes or upon the death of one of its owner(s).

A corporation can be classified as a C-Corp or as an S-Corp.

<u>C - Corporations</u>

A C-Corporation is a state-chartered business that is owned by stock holders. No stock holder is personally liable for the debts of the corporation. Legal control of the C-Corp resides with the stock holders. The stock holders may or may not be responsible for day-to-day operations of the business; they delegate a board of directors and officers of the company. Corporations must file corporate tax returns to report the corporation's income or losses. Income to officers is typically W2 income that must be shown on the IRS 1040 tax return of each officer. Because a C-corporation must pay income taxes on its corporate profits, and income paid to its owners is also taxed, it is considered to have a double tax.

The C-Corp's taxes must be reported on an IRS Form 1120.

## S Corporations

An S-Corp is only a tax election, allowing its shareholders to treat earnings and profits as distributions and have them pass through directly to each of their personal tax returns via a schedule K. S-Corps do not pay income taxes. However there is a minor catch, if a shareholder is working for the company and there is profit (key words) the shareholder (you) must pay themselves "reasonable compensation." Obviously compensation can vary from state to state as well as for the duties and services performed. The IRS rule is you must pay yourself what you would pay someone else to do your job, provided there is enough profit to do so. If you do not do this the IRS can reclassify all of your profit and earnings as wages, making you liable for all the payroll taxes on the total amount of wages and earnings reclassified.

An S-Corp is a pass through tax entity, because the income or losses are passed through to your 1040's. An S-Corp pays no taxes as an entity itself, all is passed through to its owners (shareholders). This theory is considered single taxation verses a C-Corp that is double taxed, both the corporation's profits, and the shareholders dividends are taxed. The term "pass through" refers to the portion of the corporation's income, losses, deductions or credits that are reported to the shareholder on Schedule K-1 and are shown by the shareholder on his or her own income tax return, it does not refer to assets distributed by the corporation to the shareholder. A distribution to a shareholder in excess of the shareholder's basis in their stock is taxed to the shareholder as a capital gain. A distribution to a shareholder under or equal to basis is a return of capital and not taxed.

For Federal income tax purposes, taxation of S corporations resembles that of partnerships. As in partnerships, the income, deductions, and tax credits of an S corporation pass through to shareholders annually, regardless of whether distributions are made. The owners are taxed on their proportionate shares of the S-Corporation's profits.

This means income is taxed at each shareholders tax level and not at a corporate level. Payments to S shareholders by the corporation are distributed tax-free to the extent that the distributed earnings were previously taxed, considered a return of investment. Also, certain corporate penalty taxes (e.g., accumulated earnings tax, personal holding company tax) and the alternative minimum tax do not apply to an S corporation.

The IRS has set up guidelines and the Internal Revenue Code states that in order to be classified as an S-Corp the following requirements must be met:

- Must be a legitimate entity, either a domestic corporation or a limited liability company.
- Must have only one class of stock.
- Must have 100 shareholders or less, no more.
- Spouses are automatically treated as a single
- shareholder. Families, defined as individuals descended from a common ancestor, plus spouses and former spouses of either the common ancestor or anyone lineally descended from that person, are considered a single shareholder as long as any family member elects such treatment.

- Shareholders must be U.S. citizens or residents, and must be physical entities (a person), so <u>corporate shareholders and partnerships are to be excluded</u>. However, certain tax-exempt corporations, notably <u>501(c)(3)</u> corporations, are permitted to be shareholders.
- Profits and losses must be allocated to shareholders <u>proportionately to each one's interest in the business.</u>

If a corporation ceases to meet the above requirements (for example, the number of shareholders exceeds 100 or an ineligible shareholder such as a nonresident alien acquires a share, or a class of stock changes due to transfers,) the corporation will lose its S corporation status and revert to being a regular C corporation.

If the corporation meets the above guidelines and chooses to be taxed as an S-Corp the shareholders must file form 2553 to elect the S-Corp status. The form 2553 must be signed by all shareholders, in a community property state the form must also be signed by the shareholders spouse as well.

The election to be taxed as an S-Corp must be made no later than the 15th day of the third month of the tax year for which the election is being made. This election may also be made at any time prior to the date.

Note: The above tax treatment is for federal income tax only. All other federal taxes such as FICA, and federal unemployment taxes remain the same. FICA will be required on only employee wages and not on distributive shares. However the IRS has the right to re-categorize distributions made to shareholder-employees as wages if they the shareholder-employee is not paid reasonable wages for the work and services they perform within the corporation's business.

Therefore most small-mid sized businesses choose <u>not to</u> be classified as a C-Corp. However, when first incorporating all business incorporate as a C-Corp and an election must be made in a timely manner to be taxed and viewed by the IRS as an S-Corp.
What if the S-Corp wants to convert back to a C-Corp? You may find out that due to changes in the tax laws you may want to convert back to a C-Corp.

Converting to a C corporation may offer a way to increase your investor base and raise capital. It also allows the business to offer a wider range of tax-deductible fringe benefits. However, I strongly recommend seeking the advice of a knowledgeable tax professional.

If decided it is in your best interest to convert back it is allowed. The IRS doesn't require any specific documentation. All that is required is for the corporation to file a statement of Revocation of the S-Corp status signed by an authorized person or agent of the corporation and attach to this statement a statement that is signed by its shareholders that own more than 50 percent of the issued and outstanding stock of the corporation. For this revocation to be accepted on the corporation's first day of the corp.'s taxable year, you must revoke the S election by the 15th day of the 3rd month of that tax year.

Both C-Corps and S-Corps are generally a corporation under the laws of the state in which the entity is organized. S corporations are separate legal entities from their shareholders, under state laws, generally provide their shareholders with the same liability protection offered to the shareholders of C corporations

To become a corporation you must file incorporation papers with the state. Most will file in the state they live in. Many people are unaware that each of the fifty states has its own unique statutes regarding corporate structuring, operational requirements, legal protection (such as the corporate veil) and personal privacy protection.
Some believe it is wise to incorporate in such states as Delaware or Nevada. The issue with incorporating out of state is that you will need to file two tax returns, one with each state. I believe the benefit of other state incorporations is to hide or mask the true owners of the corporation. Again most businesses choose to incorporate in the state they choose to do business in.

A corporation gives protection to its owners in the fact they are separate. The corporation is a legal entity all on its own. The corporations can own real estate, property, a corporation can open bank accounts with the corporate identity, and corporations can also borrower money. The owners are typically protected from law suits and liabilities by the corporate veil. There are times that the corporate veil maybe pierced.

Incorporating in the state of Nevada is often chosen because statistically it has rarely allowed corporate veil piercing, thus adding additional protection to the corporate owners. In the state of Nevada, the corporate veil may be pierced only if the owner of a company is found to have committed deliberate fraud. The corporate veil may be pierced more easily in other states.

The cost for incorporating is priced by each state. Most often a business will hire an attorney or other professional to prepare and file the corporate documents. Some tax professionals offer this service. You will also need to choose a registered agent for the company. A registered agent is the person who receives all documents pertaining to the corporation. A registered agent maybe a business owner, attorney or tax professional.

A corporation is required to hold an annual meeting. You will need to keep a record of the annual meeting. A board of directors also needs to be chosen. A corporate seal is typically not necessary but an added cost if you choose to use one.

An S-Corp can own a C-Corp, but a C-Corp cannot own an S-Corp.

A corporation issues stock to its owners and shareholders. A shareholder/owner must receive dividends according to the number of shares owned –regardless of the time, work or effort put forth in the business. They may also receive a return of capital, money or value put into the business.

Most states allow a single owner, Massachusetts requires two members. A married couple can account for this by naming a spouse on the corporation.

1244 Small Business Stock

This stock may be issued in a Domestic Corporation.

When starting a business you can choose to issue stock certificates for 1244 stock. It must be recorded as to the ownership of the 1244 stock. The stock must be issued in exchange for money or property, other than stock or securities.

Losses on Section 1244 (Small Business) Stock
You can deduct as an **ordinary loss**, rather than as a capital loss, a loss on the sale, trade, or worthlessness of section 1244 stock. Report the loss on Form 4797, Sales of Business Property, line 10.
Gain recognized ona section 1244 stock is a capital gain if the stock is a capital asset in your hands.. Report the gain on Schedule D (Form 1040).

When calculating a net operating loss, any ordinary loss from the sale of section 1244 stock is a business loss.

Ordinary loss limit

The amount that you can deduct as an ordinary loss is limited to $50,000 each year. On a joint return the limit is $100,000, even if only one spouse has this type of loss. If your loss is $125,000 and your spouse has no loss, you can deduct $100,000 as an ordinary loss on a joint return. The remaining $25,000 is a capital loss.

In order to treat the loss as oridiary loss you must be the original owner of the stock issued and the oerson claiming the loss. To claim a deductible loss on stock issued to your partnership, you must have been a partner when the stock was issued and have remained so until such time of the loss.

The corporation must be an operational company.

If the stock was issued before July 19, 1984, the stock must be common stock. If issued after July 18, 1984, the stock may be either common or preferred.

During its 5 most recent tax years before the loss, this corporation must have derived more than 50% of its gross receipts from other than royalties, rents, dividends, interest, annuities, and gains from sales and trades of stocks or securities. If the corporation was in existence for at least 1 year, but less than 5 years, the 50% test applies to the tax years ending before the loss. If the corporation was in existence less than 1 year, the 50% test applies to the entire period the corporation was in existence before the day of the loss.

However, if the corporation's deductions (other than the net operating loss and dividends received deductions) were more than its gross income during this period, this 50% test does not apply.

Advantages of a Corporation

- A corporation may deduct the cost of benefits it provides to its officers and employees
- Shareholders/owners (you) have limited liability for the corporation's debts/judgments against the corporation.
- Corporations are allowed to raise capitol through the sale of their stock Shareholders are only accountable for their investment in stock

of the company.

- Officers, shareholders, owners can all be held personally liable for their actions, such as failure to withhold and pay employment taxes.

- A C-Corporation can elect to choose S corporation status, this election enables company to be taxed as a pass through entity. (single tax vs. double tax)

Disadvantages of a Corporation

- Incorporation is more costly and more work involved, most often requires a professional to assist with preparation of the documents. Also requires money for filing fees.

- Corporations are monitored by federal, state and some local agencies, and as a result you must file an annual report, to comply with regulations.

- More tax forms to complete typically need a professional tax preparer.

- Incorporating as a C-Corp may result in higher overall taxes. Dividends are paid to shareholders and are not deductible from business income; thus double taxation. Most small to mid sized businesses choose to be an S-Corp. due to tax benefits.

Federal Tax Forms for "C" Corporations

- Form 1120 or 1120-A: Corp. Income Tax Return
- Form 1120-W Estimated Tax for Corporation

- Form 8109-B Deposit Coupon
- Form 4625 Depreciation
- Employment Tax Forms
- Other forms as needed for capital gains, sale of assets, alternative minimum tax, etc.

Federal Tax Forms for "S" Corporations

- Form 1120S: Income Tax Return for S Corporation
- 1120S K-1: Shareholder's Share of Income, Credit, Deductions
- Form 4625 Depreciation
- Employment Tax Forms
- Form 1040: Individual Income Tax Return
- Schedule E: Supplemental Income and Loss
- Schedule SE: Self-Employment Tax
- Form 1040-ES: Estimated Tax for Individuals

Other forms as needed for capital gains, sale of assets, alternative minimum tax, etc.

## Partnerships

- In a General Partnership, two or more people share ownership of a single business. There is no distinguishing between the business and its owners, similar to a sole proprietorship. There are three kinds of partnerships. The two most common are a General Partnership and Limited Liability Partnership, LLP.

Types of Partnerships are:

- General Partnership
  In a general partnership there will be a general partner and others that will share the profit or loss based on their agreement. Equal shares are to be assumed unless there is a written agreement that states otherwise. A General Partnerships can be formed by an oral agreement between two people or more, but a legal partnership agreement is highly recommended for either partnership.
- Limited Liability Partnership, LLP
  Limited Liability Partnership means that most of the partners have limited liability, to the extent of their investment. They also have limited participation regarding management decisions. Forming a limited partnership is more involved and slightly more complex than the forming of a general partnership.

- Joint Venture
  Acts like a general partnership, but is defined for a set period of time or a single project. If partners in a joint venture repeat the activity, they will be recognized as an ongoing partnership. They will have to file their federal taxes as well as distribute accumulated partnership assets upon dissolution of the entity.

Once you've decided on the type of partnership you would like to establish you should consider a business partnership agreement, similar to a pre-nuptial agreement. This is a written agreement signed and recorder by all parties. Any partnership should have a legal agreement between all partners that outlines how decisions will be made, how profits and losses will be shared. A plan to handle disputes when they arise, how partners can be bought out, new ones brought in, and in a worst case how to dissolve the partnership.

The business partnership agreement should include the following:

- The business name, structure, and partner information such as name, address and social security numbers, percentage of ownership, how much time and capital will be contributed.

- Description of the type of business that will be conducted

- Who will make decisions, how will duties and responsibilities be shared, as well as any limitations imposed on partners.

- Detailed outline of proposed future contributions or liabilities to be taken on by each partner

- What percentage of profits and losses will be allowed by each partner?

- A plan for dissolution, or the death of a partner, and an exit strategy for each partner.

- The amount of insurance to be carried on each partner and who the beneficiary is. This is an important decision, if not handled correctly you could end up in partnership with a deceased partner's spouse, or other family member.

As a business entity, the partnership itself does not pay taxes - each partner pays federal, state, and local taxes on their income from the partnership as if it were personal income.

General Partnership

In a General Partnership every partner has the right to manage the business and control the business. Each partner is liable for the debt of the entire business and responsible for the actions of the other partner. The disadvantage of this type of partnership is if one partner messes up all partners are responsible and pay the price for what one does.

A general partnership is dissolved immediately upon the death of any of the partner's involved – although the personal liability to partnership creditors exists even after the dissolution of the partnership.

In a Limited Liability Partnership, also know as an LLP, each partner is liable only for the amount he or she invested in the partnership. In a limited partnership, the general partner manages and controls the business, while the limited partners have no right to manage or control the business. They do get gains or losses. In the case of a limited partner's death, the partnership would remain intact. Each partner pays individual taxes on their proportionate share of net partnership income.

A partnership must file an IRS 1065 Form for the partnership. An IRS Schedule K1, Partners Share of

Income, Credits, Deductions, etc. must be filed for each partner and attached to the 1065 IRS Form. A copy is given to each partner for calculating income or loss to be reported on their schedule E, Supplemental Income and Loss, along with their 1040 personal tax return. The schedule E flows through to the 1040, thus making a partnership a pass through entity as well.

Partnerships also need to file an annual "information return" to report income, deductions, gains, losses, etc. with the IRS.

A LLP may also act separately from its owners in owning real estate, property, and borrowing money.

You should file for a city or village business license.

A bank account may also be opened by a partnership, using the partnership documents.

*Note- a partnership will automatically come into existence when two or more people come together to earn a profit and don't incorporate or form an LLC or LLP, and are not spouses. Therefore if you are running a business together with someone else right now, unless you filed to incorporate or an LLC you are a partnership.

A partnership maybe owned by an individual, a corporation or another partnership, this is called tiered structuring and becomes very tricky with taxes. The tired structuring also makes it more difficult for the IRS as well.

Advantages of a Partnership

- Partnerships are relatively simple to start

- A pass through entity – allowing both profit and loss to pass to the partner's tax returns.

- Having more than one owner gives greater insight to different business strategies
- An incentive to become a partner may also be advantageous to potential employees given the option

Disadvantages of a Partnership

- Profits and losses must be shared with other partners.

- Disagreements may occur over business decisions.

- In a general partnership all partners are jointly and individually liable for the actions of the other partners. Not so for Limited Liability Partnership

- Some employee benefits are not deductible from business income on tax returns.

- The partnership may have a controlled life; it may end upon the withdrawal or death of a partner.

Federal Tax Forms for Partnerships:

- Form 1065: Partnership Return of Income Form 1065 K-1: Partner's Share of Income, Credit, Deductions

- Form 4562: Depreciation

- Form 1040: Individual Income Tax Return

- Schedule E: Supplemental Income and Loss

- Schedule SE: Self-Employment Tax

- Form 1040-ES: Estimated Tax for Individuals

- Employment Tax Forms

Regardless of which business entity you choose, starting your own business is a wise move. Reasons to consider when defining your businesses' entity are:

- Tax advantageous and disadvantageous

- Protecting personal assets – we are in a litigious society and law suits are common place. Protect what you have worked for, make sure you have insulated yourself and put up proper barriers of protection.

- Building business strength that will enhance your chances of obtaining future credit from local banks, credit cards, unsecured business lines of credit

- Choosing an entity properly will also enhance your professionalism. Clients like to work with successful businesses and professional people. Enhance your business appearance with the proper entity.

**Applying for an EIN number**

Every business should have an EIN number. An EIN number is a nine-digit number used by the IRS to identify each business. It helps the IRS keep track of who is filing what. EIN number's are used by all entities, sole proprietors, corporations, partnerships, LLC's, and non-for profit organizations.

Use your EIN number on all correspondence with the IRS. An EIN number should most often be used in place of your social security number.

You need to complete form SS-4 ( also found on IRS.gov website) to obtain an EIN number. You can also call 1-800-TAX –FORMS to request the form and instructions by mail. Your EIN number is a personal number, keep it private.

You can apply online for an EIN number. You can also mail, call or fax information in for an EIN number. Go to IRS.GOV and type in EIN form and the proper form should pop up. In order to use the online application the business must be located here in the United States

Once you complete all information requested, and it is validated you will be given you EIN number on line immediately. To obtain by phone you can call the toll free number 1-800-829-4933) If you have form SS-4 completed prior to calling it will make it a little easier.

To obtain by fax you will complete and fax SS-4 form. You will fax your form to the number listed for your state. This number can be looked up at IRS.Gov It should take approximately 4 days. Be sure to include either your fax number or email address to receive your EIN number quickly.

When filing by mail be prepared to wait up to 4 weeks. An EIN number is available to all entities. To mail or fax your application you can print a PDF application. Complete and mail or fax. The process of obtaining an EIN number is easy, quick and FREE!

# IRS Approved Home-Based

# Business Deductions

**The Home-Based Business Guide:**
**IRS Approved Home-Based Business Deductions**

Technology is making it easier than ever for people to operate a business out of their house, many taxpayers may be able to qualify for the home office business deductions when filing their federal tax returns.

The U.S. tax code is extremely complicated which is why many small businesses, home-based businesses and individuals make mistakes in their accounting, recordkeeping and filing of their returns. It is so important to work with a professional that understands the rules.

The IRS has many allowable *legitimate* business deductions for the home-based business owner. Understanding the difference between a credit and a deduction is also very helpful.

Planning is a key approach to keeping most of your hard earned dollars in your pockets vs. Uncle Sam's. Start planning immediately to avoid costly mistakes later and maximize your deduction power to reduce your tax liability.

It was during the late 1700's that Great Britain imposed taxes on the colonies, the Sugar Act in 1764, the Stamp Act in 1765, and the Tea Act in 1773. The colonies thought these taxes were unfair because the colonies did not have a representative or voice in the British Parliament when these laws were passed. This led the colonies to demand "no taxation without representation," which we still believe in today.

Did you know? If you pay someone to prepare your tax return, choose your preparer wisely. Taxpayers are legally responsible for what's on their own tax returns even if prepared by someone else. So, it is important to choose a qualified tax professional when hiring an individual or firm to prepare your tax returns, personal or business. Unqualified tax preparers may overlook legitimate deductions or credits that could cause clients to pay more tax than they should. Unqualified preparers may also make costly mistakes causing their clients to incur assessed deficiencies, penalties, and interest.

Many tax professionals understand the basics, some know how to enter your information into a data base or tax program, but there is more to being a true tax professional than entering information into a program.

The U.S. tax code can be very complicated, which is why many small businesses and home-based business may make a mistake in their book keeping and tax planning. If the tax professional understands the IRS rules and codes they will guide you more appropriately in your business.

Only attorneys, CPAs and enrolled agents can represent taxpayers before the IRS in all matters including audits, collection actions and appeals. The tax payer need not be present; it may be beneficial but not required. Other return preparers may represent taxpayers only in audits regarding a return that they signed as a preparer and with the taxpayer present.

An attorney may know some of the rules if they specialize in taxes and the same for the CPA. An Enrolled Agent on the other hand must pass rigorous federal tests provided by the IRS. Upon successfully passing the tests in all three areas of the U.S. tax code; their application to practice before the IRS will be reviewed and examined by the IRS, Office of Professional Responsibility. Once this is complete the enrolled agent is granted approval from the IRS, and *"admitted to practice before the IRS."* This is very important if you should be audited, assessed a tax penalty incorrectly, or a lien/levy placed against you. An enrolled agent is federally authorized to represent you any where in the country before the IRS.

You may also want to find out if your tax preparer is affiliated with a professional organization that provides or requires its members to pursue continuing education and holds them accountable to a code of ethics. Some examples of such organizations would be:

- National Association of Tax Professionals
- National Association of Enrolled Agents

- National Association of Tax consultants
- The American Institute of Certified Public Accountants
- State Bar Association (attorneys)
- Enrolled Agents of America (LinkedIn Group only)

Another key to consider in choosing a preparer is to find a professional that specializes in what you do. A qualified professional should:

- Help you plan your tax strategy early

- Re-evaluate current tax situation annually
- Assist you in financial questions and life changing events

- Stay on top of changes

They should also be familiar with your type of business, possess a comfort level with your income, not to high, not to low, just right.

An IRS agent once said, "You don't want a tax professional, (CPA, accountant, attorney, or enrolled agent) that lies, nor do you want one that talks you into filing an overly conservative return.

Many taxpayers have a fear of being audited, whether they choose to be aggressive or non-aggressive in their returns they still have the same fear. There are some triggers that can cause an IRS audit. Statistically it has been noted that the combination of: a home-based business and a Schedule C have the highest chance of an audit.  A corporation has the least chance of an audit, with a C-Corp less than an S-Corp.  Estates are rarely audited.

Knowing this in advance allows you to carefully plan your business strategy so it is allowing you maximum tax benefits while being 100% IRS compliant.  This calls for a shrewd tax professional.

Whomever you choose make sure they mirror your ethics and professionalism, and remember a paid preparer must sign the return as required by law as the preparer and must also include their Preparer Tax ID Number, PTIN. Keep in mind that although the tax preparer signs your return, you are responsible for the accuracy of every item on your return. In addition, the preparer must furnish you a copy of your tax return prior to but no later than upon you signing the return.

Most return preparers are professional, honest and provide excellent service to their clients.

No tax professional will ever know what you know about your business.  It is up to you to share this information making you the most valuable asset in your tax planning. It makes no difference to the IRS whether you run your business form home or from an outside office or workplace - either way you are able to deduct business expenses.

Do you know the difference between a deduction and a tax credit?

A deduction (expense, write-off) is taken after establishing gross income.  Once gross income is determined all allowable deductions applicable will reduce gross income thus giving you adjusted gross income. Your Income tax is then determined on your adjusted gross income, therefore by reducing your gross income you will reduce your tax liability.

You are only obligated to pay taxes on your adjusted gross income.

Gross income
-deductions
=Adjusted Gross Income

So they key for all business owners (home-based or not) is to reduce gross income, thus lowering your adjusted gross income, resulting in lowering YOUR taxes.

There are three types of deductions available: personal, business and investment. We will be discussing business deductions only.

A credit is given on taxes you owe, for example when your tax returns were completed you would owe the IRS $3000 before any credits are used. A credit reduces the tax liability you owe. Many will only allow you to reduce it to zero; very few will allow you to reduce beyond zero. One that will is the First Time Home Buyers Credit. This credit will allow you up to 8000.00 in credit so using the above example of owing $3000.00 you would get $5000 back. If you owed zero you would get $8000.00 back. There are guidelines and rules for this credit.
We will be discussing deductions primarily. All home based businesses have some kind of expenses, therefore deductions.

The IRS has set guidelines in order to qualify as a home-based business; here is what the IRS Code looks for when you are claiming home office deductions.

In order to claim a home-based business deduction for your home, you must use part of your home exclusively and regularly:

- As your principal place of business, or

- As a place to meet or deal with patients, clients or customers in the normal course of your business, or

- If a separate structure exists that is not attached to your home, it must be used in connection with your trade or business

Home-office deduction

The amount you are allowed to deduct is based on the percentage of your home that you used for business. The home-office deduction is depreciation of your home and operating expenses, like utilities. You will need to determine the amount of square footage used for your business.

This can easily be done, first figure out the total amount of square footage of your home's living space. Next divide the square footage of your office space by the total space of living space. The percentage is the amount that is deductible for your home-based business. The same percentage is also deductible for all utility bills as well.

The IRS is very specific about the space only being

used for business. You cannot use a closet or bookshelves for personal use; it must all be used for business in the designated room or area in order to qualify for the deduction.

Some preparers feel this isn't a wise decision to use your depreciation as a deductible now. It has an affect on capital gains when selling your home. It is also believed that the presence of form 8829 used to claim your home-office deduction is a red flag to the IRS agents due to home-office abuse. This is where you need to have a discussion with your tax professional to determine what is best for you.

Business Deductions and Expenses

To qualify the expense must be ordinary and necessary, current, directly related to your business and reasonable in amount. (IRC 162) Expenses (deductions) can include the following items: home office expenses, equipment rental, legal and accounting fees, car and truck expenses, meal and entertainment, supplies and materials, publications, repair and maintenance, business taxes, interest on business loans, licenses, banking fees, advertising costs, business related education, postage, professional dues, business liability and property insurance, and payments to independent contractors are most of them.

Some deductions for certain expenses will be limited if your gross income from your business is less than your total business expenses.

Business trips: transportation expenses such as car rental, bus, plane, boat, taxi or automotive expenses in addition to tolls and parking fees. These expenses are treated as travel expenses if you stayed away from home overnight, Otherwise they will be considered transportation expenses.

Many pleasure trips may be turned in to a business trip as well. It is not necessary to spend your whole time working but if you can document that you made business contacts, maybe did a little research relevant to your business you will be able to deduct some of the cost of your trip. The percentage of the trip that was used for business.

Auto Expenses

You can deduct the cost of operating and maintaining your car when traveling away from home on business. You can choose between actual expenses or the standard mileage rate as a deduction. You are also able to deduct business-related tolls and parking. If you use a rental car d while away from home on business, you can deduct only the business-use portion of the expenses.

Mileage

The IRS has ruled that as a home-based business owner you can deduct the expense of the first mile from home each ay. So plan a trip every time you go out to include a business function. Stopping at the post office, PO Box, visiting clients, printing, banking all are legitimate business stops.

Mileage may be deductible if you have another job. If you drive to your first job first and then later drive to sell or market your home-based business the mileage is deductible.

The standard mileage rate for 2009, beginning on January 1$^{st}$ is .55 cents per mile driven for the use of cars, pick-up trucks, SUV's or a van.

Parking Fees

Fees paid to park at your workplace are not deductible, but you can deduct business-related parking fees when visiting a client or customer place of business.

Auto Depreciation

There are a few different ways you may be able to depreciate your car when used for business.

You have the option of choosing the standard mileage deduction per business mile, or you can take actual (real) expenses, including depreciation. You are not allowed depreciation together with the standard mileage deduction.

You will be allowed to switch between the two and you are switching from standard to actual it will change the type of depreciation you will be allowed to take. You will have to take a straight line of depreciation.

A key factor to know is when a car is owned by a corporation, 100% of the costs can be deducted. Remember any personal use you as an employee of the corporation use the car for has to be included as taxable income.

Education - A taxpayer can deduct education costs if they meet one of the following:

The education is required by employer or the law to keep present salary, status or job. The education must serve as a bona fide business "purpose" to employer

OR

The education maintains or improves skills needed in the taxpayer's PRESENT work.

Entertainment

It's ok that you don't have an outside office; you still may do a large portion of your business away from your home-office. Many important business meetings, marketing ideas, networking and sales often happen at restaurants, golf courses and sports events.

Entertainment is deductible up to 50%, provided they are ordinary and necessary business activities. Expenses included in the 50% deductions would be:

- Meals & Entertainment
- Tax & Tips related to business meal
- Cover charges for admissions to night clubs
- Rent for room in which taxpayer holds a dinner or cocktail party
- Parking at a sports arena

What constitutes business entertainment? There are two tests to consider, the directly related theory or the associated test.

Directly-Related theory is the entertainment must be directly related and take place in a true business setting for business purposes, and then the expenses will be deemed related to your business.  Some examples of business venues would be:

- hospitality rooms at conventions
- restaurants, cafes, pubs, buffets, supper clubs
- coffee shops

To be considered directly related:

- The main purpose of the entertainment and business was to conduct business discussions.
- You must engage in conversation and business discussions with the person during the entertainment period.
- Your intention was to gain additional business sometime in the future or some other specific business benefit.

All provide a good setting to meet and discuss business services and products.

Not-directly related entertainment expenses considered to not be directly related are:

- If you personally are not present at the event

- In situations that offer distractions that more than likely will cause you to be distracted and prevent you from conducting business as you would in a directly related setting.

Examples of not direct related locations or events that would cause a high level of distraction would be:

- Nightclubs, theatres, sporting events
- Social gatherings such as a cocktail party
- Cocktail lounges, golf clubs, athletic clubs or vacation resorts

However the IRS states that they could be deductible expenses if you are entertaining guests at nightclubs, social, athletic and sporting clubs, at theatres, sporting events, on yachts, hunting, and fishing. Entertainment typically is any activity considered to provide entertainment, recreation or amusement.

You also have what is called an associated test, so if you expenses do not meet the directly-related test, they may meet the associated test. To meet the associated test you need to show the entertainment is related to your active trade or business AND directly before or after the event a noteworthy business discussion took place.

An expense is considered associated with your business if you can show that your intentions were truly business minded. The intention may be to obtain new business or keep and foster existing business.

A business discussion is considered to be substantial if you personally engage in the discussion, meeting, presentation, negotiation, training or other business activity to provide a business benefit.

There is no set time for the length of the discussion nor do you have to spend more time discussing business than entertaining, you just need to show it was substantial to the business.

If the meeting takes place at a convention or like event that is sponsored by a professional organization or business it is considered to be a substantial business meeting. The reason for your attendance must be to increase or further your trade or business.

Business and entertainment on hunting, fishing, or on yachts and other pleasure boats are not considered to be the main purpose for business, even if you are able t o show that business was the main purpose generally you cannot deduct these expenses.

Who can you can claim as a business contact or associate:

- Clients: patrons or consumers
- Suppliers
- Customers
- Independent Contractors
- Agents
- Partners
- Professional advisors, (including your tax professional)

As a taxpayer you are not required to show that business income or other business benefits actually derived from entertainment expenses; however you are required to show that you did engage in business with the other party during the entertainment period. The taxpayer must believe that it will bring increased business income or benefit some time in the future. Entertainment can be deducted at 50%

Entertainment can include meals you provide to your customers or clients. You must be present at the time the meal is served or provided.

A meal can be expensed either as part of entertainment or by itself.

Dining/Meals - If you take clients or perspective clients to lunch or dinner you can claim a business deduction. A meal includes the food, beverages, taxes and tips. Either you or your employee must be present. Meal/dining expenses are subject to the 50% rule limit.

The IRS doesn't require receipts for meals and entertainment expenses that are less than $75.00.
It is easy to misinterpret rule.

The IRS clearly states that you need to document/have a record of where you went, who you went with, what you discussed, and the relationship with the person you were with. A receipt is easier! Jot down the information requested on the back and you have done what was requested. Ideally a credit card receipt works best. A receipt is often easier to keep than an extensive log. I suggest keeping an envelope or box in your car, this way you can write on it and toss it in the designated envelope or box. Women can have a special organizer in their purse, either can have an organizer for receipts in a brief case as well.

Family Help – Employing your children or parents!

Hiring family members is an advantage of operating your own business. Employment tax varies for different family members.

Standard employment taxes include the following taxes:
Federal income tax withholding (FITW)
Social Security and Medicare taxes (FICA)
Federal unemployment taxes (FUTA)

Children Employed by Parents

If the child is under age 18 and works for his/her parent in a trade or business would not be subject to social security or Medicare taxes, if the parents owned the business as a sole proprietorship or a partnership that each partner is a parent of the child.

If the child is under age 21 and works for his/her parent in a trade or business would not be subject to Federal Unemployment Tax (FUTA), income for services rendered by the child are subject to income tax with holding, regardless of age.
The wages for the services of a child are subject to income tax withholding as well as social security, Medicare, and FUTA taxes if the following business entity exists, a corporation, owned and controlled by the child's parent or a partnership, regardless of the child's parent being a *partner. If the child works for an estate, even when the estate is the estate of a deceased parent income tax withholding as well as social security, Medicare, and FUTA taxes are withheld.

*Unless each partner is a parent of the child.

## Spouse employed by other spouse

When one spouse works for another in a trade or business their wages are subject to income tax withholding, social security and Medicare taxes, but not to FUTA tax, when a sole proprietor.

The wages for services of a spouse when working for a corporation, controlled or not by the other spouse, or a partnership, even if the other spouse is a partner is subject are subject to income tax withholding, social security, Medicare, and FUTA taxes.

## Parent employed by child

If your parent works for you in your business, the wages you pay to him or her are subject to income tax withholding and social security and Medicare taxes, not FUTA tax, regardless of the type of service performed.

## Office Expenses:

- furniture: desks, bookcases, chairs
- equipment: faxes, computer, monitor, etc
- Both furniture and equipment may be expensed after start up year. Many of these items will be considered a capitol expense, which means it has a useful life of more than one year. All furniture and equipment can be depreciated from the first time you use them through out there depreciatory life span.
- supplies:  paper, envelopes, pens,

- personal business information – are deducted in the year purchased
- personnel: salaries – deducted in the year paid

Section 179

Section 179 of the IRS tax code was created to help business owners. The Economic Stimulus Act of 2008 included special provisions for Section 179, and greatly increased the limits on how much businesses can deduct. The American Recovery and Reinvestment Act of 2009 extended those provisions until the end of the year, December 31$^{st}$, 2009. Section 179 allows businesses to deduct the full purchase price for new equipment including computers, up to $250,000.00 to be deductible, regardless of the size of your company as long as it is purchased before December 31$^{st}$, 2009.

This was done to spur on the economy and get business owners to invest in their businesses and get more money back in their pockets by doing so. The amount for 2009 tax year is up to $250,000, (plus 50% bonus depreciation). This amount is almost double to previous years before 2008. Section 179 is a great incentive for home-based businesses to purchase or lease equipment this year.

This allows the home-based business owner to take the deduction on equipment purchased now for the full amount of the purchase price (maximum $250,000.00) on this year's tax return instead of amortizing it over fifteen years. What this means is if you purchase (or lease) qualifying equipment, you CAN deduct the whole purchase price form your gross income.

In 2009 you are allowed to deduct up to $105,000.00 for computers and computer related equipment. By deducting the full cost, you lower the amount you pay for equipment or computer substantially.

You can only deduct an amount equal to the amount of your net income. For example your net income is $25,000.00 then you can deduct up to $25,000.00. You must choose to use the section 179 deduction rather than amortize (depreciate) your purchase of an extended period of time.

Most equipment qualifies. Guideline is if you use it for business, more than likely it will qualify. The equipment MUST be put into use between January 1, 2009 and December 31$^{st}$, 2009. The following is a list of equipment: (must be used for business)

- Equipment/machinery
- Tangible real (personal) property
- Business vehicles with gross weight in excess of 6000 lbs
- Office Furniture
- Office Equipment: fax, phone, scanner, etc.
- Computers
- Computer Software
- Property attached to your building that is not structural: car wash equipment, printing press...
- Partial business, partial personal must be prorated for business usage.

There is a list posted by the IRS, qualifying Section 179 equipment. You can go to www.irs.gov and type Section 179 equipment in, you should be able to find it from there.

This is the best time to take advantage of Section 179 deductions. These rules for Section 179 can change so make your purchases this year!

There may be instances however that you may choose not to use Section 179 deductions. It needs to be planned out by a tax professional. You don't want to be paying for equipment three to five years from now, with no deductions available to you.

Insurance Premiums – medical, dental, vision and long term care insurance are allowable deduction for you and your family, as a sole proprietor, partner in partnership or member of an LLC.

Operating Expenses - Rent, mortgage, utilities: gas, electric, phone, and water these are done on a proportionate basis depending on the amount of your home you use for the business. These are all deductible in the year incurred.

You can deduct the portion of your home that you use for business; it will be based on the amount of square footage used. You are also entitled to the same proportionate share of utilities as well.

The only drawback with claiming a room as a home-based business deduction, is when you sell your property you must not include the income from that percentage point, ex. 25% of your home is used for business, when selling 25% of the sale and profit will be earmarked to go as income property and you will pay capitol gains if there are any, no deduction is allowed.

On all primary residence you are allowed a deduction of up to $250,000.00/single and $500,000.00/married filing jointly as an offset to your taxable gain.

Retirement plans – are a great way to save for your future. You can save money and not pay income taxes on it as well, as long as you are putting the correct amount of funds into a "qualified" tax plan. A qualified plan is in compliance with the IRS requirements. Traditional IRS's and 401K's are considered qualified, Roth IRA's and 401K's are not.

Vehicle – you are entitled to deduct the interest you pay on your automotive loans if you use them for business. If your use is 100% you can deduct 100% of the interest, if you use it 75% for business and 25% for personal then you can only deduct 75% of the interest.

It doesn't matter whether you deduct your automotive expenses using the standard mileage rate or the actual mileage rate. You are allowed to use the standard mileage deduction per business mile, or you are allowed to take the actual expenses, including depreciation.

You can switch between the two methods, however once you start with the standard mileage and you want to switch to actual expenses, you must use a straight line depreciation system verses the modified accelerated cost recovery system commonly known as MACRS.
If your car is owned by the corporation, 100% of the costs can be deducted. Keep in mind any personal use will need to be included as taxable income to you.

Business Gifts

Business gifts you give away in the normal course of business are deductible up to $25.00 that you give to each person either directly or indirectly.

When giving a gift to a company it is considered to be an indirect gift to a particular person or class of people.

If you choose to give a gift to a client or customer's family, the gift is also considered an indirect gift.

Gifts given by you nd your spouse are considered to be one, it doesn't matter if you have two different business relationships it is still considered as a gift from one taxpayer.

Exceptions to the rule

There is an exception to the $25.00 rule, the exception is an item that costs less than $4.00 or less and:

Has your name permanentley imprinted on the gift and Is one of a numebr of identical items you widely distribute, such as bags, pens, magnets, etc

Also excluded are signs , display racks, or other promitional material to be used on the business premises of the reciepent of the item.

If you choose to be generous and give more costly gifts that's ok, just know that only the first $25.00 of each gift to each customer or client will be deductible.

Reimbursable Business Expenses

Often times small business owners and home-based business owners will pay for business expenses out of their own pockets or with personal credit cards. These expenses can be reimbursed by your company.

The key is to keep track of the expenditures and good records. Your company should have a written policy in place establishing a plan for deductions and reimbursement to be non-taxable to employees.

If you don't keep track you can still claim un-reimbursed business expenses n your personal tax returns, Schedule A, but your expenses must exceed 2% of your adjusted gross income to qualify as a deduction.

Business Start-up Costs

Home based businesses are also allowed to deduct business start up costs during the first year of up to $5,000.00 any amount over 5000.00 will need to be spread out of the next 15 years – amortized/capitalized.

Allowable home-based business's start up costs:

- Legal fees; Tax professional/attorney fees/start up - business entity costs
- Market research
- City/village license fees
- Advertising & marketing
- Office furniture, equipment & supplies
- Operation costs
- Cost of inventory
- Capital expenses

## Gifts

The IRS allows you to deduct up to $25.00 per person per year. If you choose to spend more, then only the first $25.00 is deductible the rest is not.

## Record Keeping and Filing Taxes

All business owners must keep accurate records that wil l show the IRS you actually spent the money. You should keep all records for a minimum of three years from the date you file your return as well as all receipts and pertinent information that goes along with each year.

Home-based and self-employed business owners are required to pay social security and Medicare taxes totaling 15.3%. Sole proprietors, partners in a partnership and a member in an LLC are all allowed to deduct one-half (7.65%) of your self-employment from your total net business income. This is an adjustment not a deduction but reduces your gross income, lowering the tax liability you would owe. If you have an employee you must pay one-half of social security and Medicare for the employee and the employee will pay the other one-half.

All home-based businesses are expected to file their tax returns on time. Most home-based businesses will either be sole proprietorships, maybe S corp., partnership or LLC. Whichever entity you have chosen a tax year is considered adopted or chosen when the first tax return is filed. Most home –based business owners will adapt a calendar year, which goes from January 1$^{st}$ until December 31$^{st}$ of the year.

A fiscal year may be chosen but is unlikely for the small home-based business. A fiscal year is twelve consecutive months ending on any month's last day except December. A fiscal year can vary from 52-53 weeks.

A business owner must also determine their method of claiming income, accrual method vs. cash method. Accrual means you can include or deduct income and expenses in the year they occurred.

A cash method means you can only include/deduct them when received.

Individual tax returns are due on April 15, can request an automatic 6 month extension. Corporate returns are due on the 15$^{th}$ day of the 3$^{rd}$ month after the end of its tax year. Partnerships are due on fifteenth day of the fourth month following the close of its fiscal year.

*All entities may be required to pay quarterly payments if income taxes owed were $1000.00 or more in previous year. *Other determining factors as well, check with your tax professional.

Tax write-offs can be a big advantage for owning a home-based business. Careful planning, organization and record keeping are essential in optimizing your benefits. Expert help is important. The cost of a good tax preparer is worth his/her weight in gold. Don't forget you get to deduct your tax preparer's fee on next year's tax returns.

A home-based business can offer a magnitude of business deductions and great tax write-offs. My recommendation is to maximize your home-based businesses success by taking the deductions you are allowed and keeping good records and documentation. Don't pass up a deduction that is legitimate for fear of an audit.

The most audited forms are schedule C ( Sole Proprietorship), Home-based business Form8829 (Home-office deduction), the combination has the highest chance of an audit. Corporations are the least audited, C-Corps less than S-Corps. Estates are the least audited. Start planning now. Now is the best time to prepare for next year's taxes. Make an appointment to discuss your home-based business's tax needs with a qualified tax professional.

**This hand book has been put together as an informative project and IN NO WAY is intended to practice Law, give legal advice or a written opinion. It is not intended as tax advice to any person or groups of individuals or business owners.**

For further information please contact:
Laura Burke, EA.
Professional Tax Masters, Inc
Offices in Chicago & New Lenox

Burke is an enrolled agent, *"admitted to practice before the IRS"*, as well as a trainer for the Illinois Tax Training Institute. Burke is available to start your business entity, prepare your tax returns or negotiate your tax matters. She is also available as a guest speaker, trainer or facilitator. www.lauralynnburke.com She may be reached at LLynn145@aol.com. 708-692-6199 Direct 708-969-2229 Office

Laura has two new books coming out Networkology™ "The power of combining traditional networking skills with technology to create award-winning relationships" *and* Stepping Stones to Success, co-authored with Jack Canfield and Deepak Chopra. You may order these books at www.networkology.net
www.Steppingstonestosuccess.name    708-743-2929

Laura Lynn Burke, EA
*"Admitted to practice before the IRS"*
Enrolled Agent - Tax Professional
Professional Tax Masters, Inc
Offices in Chicago & New Lenox  708-969-2229
OFFICE    708-692-6199 CELL